A BIBLICAL ACCOUNT of WHAT GOD'S WORD TEACHES ABOUT CHRIST

DR. JOHN THOMAS WYLIE

authorHOUSE®

AuthorHouse™
1663 Liberty Drive
Bloomington, IN 47403
www.authorhouse.com
Phone: 1 (800) 839-8640

Published by AuthorHouse 03/05/2018

ISBN: 978-1-5462-3211-7 (sc)
ISBN: 978-1-5462-3210-0 (e)

Print information available on the last page.

King James Version (KJV)
Public Domain

New International Version (NIV)
*Holy Bible, New International Version®, NIV® Copyright ©1973, 1978, 1984,
2011 by Biblica, Inc.® Used by permission. All rights reserved worldwide.*

Revised Standard Version (RSV)
*Revised Standard Version of the Bible, copyright © 1946, 1952, and 1971 the
Division of Christian Education of the National Council of the Churches of
Christ in the United States of America. Used by permission. All rights reserved.*

New American Standard Bible (NASB)
*Copyright © 1960, 1962, 1963, 1968, 1971, 1972, 1973,
1975, 1977, 1995 by The Lockman Foundation*

CONTENTS

INTRODUCTION

There is the indistinguishable connection between being in close association with Christ and the yearning to convey individuals to salvation. Those of us who take after Christ need others to follow Him moreover. Ordinarily they feel deficient in arrangement or an absence of certainty to talk up for Christ for dread they may neglect to answer the protests or reactions. Bringing the Good News of salvation through confidence, faith and the Lord Jesus Christ is additionally the last prerequisite of the Savior to the majority of His Church.

It is the plan of this publication to: "Go ye into all the world and broadcast, report, teach and proclaim the Gospel." It is the obligation of each Christian. As Christians, we are called to speak to and display Christ. It is here that we concentrate on the Biblical record of what God's Word teaches about Christ.

Why the Bible? Since it is the Christian's Holy Book from God (Scriptures) in which we discover a record of what God has done and declared in history for his picked individuals and for all of humankind, and what God requires of men in light of what he has done that they might be saved.

It is the main answer for the wrongdoing (sin) and despondency of humanity and the main route for compromise with God for everlasting life (Romans 6:23; John 3:36; 3:16).

Majority of scriptures are taken from the King James Version, The New Life Version, American Standard Version, and "Paraphrased," unless otherwise indicated.

Reverend Dr. John Thomas Wylie

CHAPTER
ONE

The Christ

The One who has been anointed (Jesus Christ). The word signifies that one has had oil rubbed upon him. The rubbing of oil on one signified that the receiver of the anointing had been chosen for a certain honor. Jesus was called "the Christ" because he was the Chosen one of the Father in heaven. In the New Testament the word is used as the Greek subsititute for the Hebrew word "Messiah."

The Christ was a term which showed that the Messiah of the Old Testament prophecies was meant (Matt.16:16; Mark 8:29; John 1:41). Jesus, the personal name given to Christ at birth, is often used with Christ – Jesus Christ – so that Christ is practically a part of the proper name of Jesus (John 1:17; Acts 11:17; Romans 5:1).

It has been suggested that the word denotes Jesus' kingly authority and mediatorial position as the "Servant of the Lord (The New Combined Bible Dictionary, 1984)."

Christ Is One Of The Three-In-One God: (Christ Always Was, Is Now, And Always Will Be)

The Word of God tells in many spots that Christ was with the Father. There has never been a period when Christ was definitely not. The initial five verses in John recount this. John 1:1-5 says, "The Word (Christ) was to start with. The Word was with God. The Word was God. He was with God first and foremost. He made all things. Nothing was made without Him making it.

Life started by Him. His Life was the Light for men. The Light sparkles in the murkiness. The obscurity has never possessed the capacity to put out the Light."

The principal verse of Genesis tells about when the world was made. As there has never been a period when God the Father was not, so there has never been a period when Christ was definitely not.

A few interpretations of the New Testament utilize the word brgotten in John 3:16. This word in the English dialect implies brought into he world or given life which would imply that Christ was not with the Father from the earliest starting point, but rather started life in Bethlehem. The Greek word implies just or just a one of a kind.

In Philippians 2:6-7 it says, "Jesus has dependably been as God seems to be. Be that as it may, He didn't hold to His rights as God. He set aside everything that had a place with Him and made Himself the same as a worker who is possessed by somebody. He ended up noticeably human by being conceived as a man." Christ was with the Father before He came as a man to live among men. Christ left paradise to result in these present circumstances world, He (as God) did not lay these things aside, but rather He didn't utilize them while He was on earth.

Hebrews 1:2-3 says, "However in these last days He has addressed us through His Son. God gave His Son everything. It was by His Son that God made the world. The Son sparkles with the sparkling enormity of the Father. The Son is as God is inside and out. The Son holds up the entire world by the energy of His Word. The Son gave His own particular life so we could be spotless from all transgression. After He had done that, He sat down on the correct side of God in Heaven."

Christ brought the world into being and keeps it by His power. In Colossians 1:16 it says that everything is for Christ and by Him. Hebrews 10:5-7 explains why Christ came to earth."

At the point when Christ went to the world, He said to God, "You don't need creatures slaughtered or blessings given in love. You have made My body prepared to give as a blessing. You are not satisfied with creatures that have been murdered or consumed and given as endowments on the sacrificial stone to take away sin.' Then I stated, "I have come to do what You need, O God. It is composed in the Law that I would."

Jesus said in John 8:58 that He was before Abraham. In John 17:5 He discussed the sparkling enormity which He had with the Father before the world was. In John 17:24 He talked about the Father's adoration for Him before the world was made. At the point when Jesus conversed with His followers in the room on the second floor before He gave His life, He stated, "I originated from the Father and have appeared on the scene. I am leaving the world and setting off to the Father." Christ was before John the Baptist (John 1:1; 17:5, 24; Colossians 1:17; Hebrews 1:2).

Christ Is One Of The Three-In-One God

Christ is One of the Three-in-one God. He is the One Who left paradise and lived in human substance. I Timothy 3:16 says, "It is vital to know the mystery of God-like living, which is: Christ came to earth as a Man. He was immaculate in His soul. He was seen by blessed messengers (angels). The countries caught wind of Him. Men wherever put their trust in Him. He was taken up into Heaven."

(Christ was the sheep of God Who was murdered for man like a sheep and given on the sacred place.). A decent man who was brimming with adoring - feel sorry for and cherishing - graciousness would not have been sufficient. Man required the Lord of paradise, the Christ Who could pay for man's transgressions with His own particular blood and set him free. Man required One Who has dependably been alive and dependably will be (Isaiah 53:6).

Making the world from nothing was the work

of Christ. John 1:3 says, "He made all things. Nothing was made without Him making it." Colossians 1:16 says, "Christ made everything in the sky and on the earth. He made everything that is seen and things that are not seen. He made every one of the forces of paradise. Everything was made." without a doubt He enteered the human family to live as a man, however this was not the start of life for Him. He generally was. All things were made by Christ and for Him. Nothing was made that He didn't make. That is the reason Christ is the Head for goodness' sake.

Christ Is Seen In The Old Testament

Christ showed Himself in Two Ways: In the Old Testament Christ is found in things and items. A portion of the things that Christ is seen in were in the Garden of Eden. Adam and Eve were permitted to see the sparkling significance of the Lord and hear the voice of the LORD GOD. "At that point they heard the sound of the Lord God strolling in the garden at night.

The man and his significant other concealed themselves from the Lord God among the trees of the garden" (Genesis 3:8). After transgression gone into the hearts of the initial two individuals, uncommon cherubim stood east of the garden of Eden holding consuming swords, "So He drove the man out. What's more, He put cherubim east of the garden of Eden with a sword of flame that turned each way."

They kept watch over the way to the tree of life" (Genesis 3:24). These were simply the ones through which Christ set aside a few minutes.

He showed Himself to Abraham before he moved to the place where there is Canaan. "Presently the Lord said to Abram, "Leave your nation, your family and your dad's home, and go to the land that I will indicate you.

What's more, I will make you an incredible country. I will convey great to you. I will make your name incredible, so you will be regarded. I will convey great to the individuals who regard you, And I will revile the individuals who revile you. Good will go to all the families of the of the earth because of you" (Genesis 12:1-3).

At the consuming hedge, Moses saw the fire and heard the voice of God. "Presently Mosses was dealing with the run of his dad in-law Jethro, the religious pioneer of Midian.

He drove the rush toward the west side of the betray, and came to Horeb, the heap of God. There the Angel of the Lord showed Himself to Moses in a consuming flame from inside a shrub.

Moses looked and saw that the shrub was consuming with flame, yet it was not being consumed. So Moses stated, "I should move to one side and see this extraordinary thing, why the shrubbery is not being consumed." The Lord saw him move to one side to look. Also, God called to him from inside the shrub, saying, "Moses, Moses!" Moses replied, "Here I am." God stated, "Don't draw close. Take your shoes off your feet. For where you are standing is sacred ground."

He said additionally, "I am the God of your father, the God of Abraham, the God of Isaac, and the God of Jacob." Then Moses shrouded his face. For he was reluctant to take a look at God" (Exodus 3:1-6)."

God could lead the Jewish individuals with a cloud amid the day and with a fire amid the night. "The Lord went before them, in a mainstay of cloud amid the day to lead them in transit, and in a mainstay of flame amid the near to give them light. So they could travel day and night. The mainstay of cloud amid the day and the mainstay of flame amid the night did not leave the general population" (Exodus 13:21-22).

The sparkling significance of God was seen when a cloud secured the place of love. At that point the clooud secured the tent. the sparkling significance of the Lord filled the sacred tent. Moses was not ready to go into the meeting tent on the grounds that the cloud had rested upon it and the sparkling enormity of the Lord filled the sacred tent. At the point when the cloud was lifted from the meeting tent, the general population of Israel would go on their way through all their voyaging days.

In any case, when the cloud was not lifted, they didn't proceed onward until the day when it was lifted. For the billow of the Lord laid on the meeting tent amid the day. Furthermore, fire was in the cloud amid the night. It was seen by all the place of Israel as they voyaged (Exodus 40:34-38)."

In these things or objects that Chrisst was seen by the people in the Old Testament times. The "Shining greatness (Or Shining

Significance) of the Lord" is a name for Christ as He was seen by men. "The Word of the Lord is a name for Christ as He was heard by men.

In the Old Testament, Christ is viewed as a man. There is a being call the Angel of Jehovah. He has the privilege and the power to do things others can not or must not do. He has the privilege to be worshiped. The Bible talks about One such Being or Angel. The One is additionally called the "Son of God" and the "Almighty God (All-powerful God).

The work done by this Angel of Jehovah is said to be simply the work of Christ (Genesis 22:1, 11, 12, 16;32:24-32).

In Micah 5:2 it shows that Christ showed Himself commonly in the good 'ol days. These circumstances when He was seen and heard in the Old Testament were as pictures of when He would come to earth in human tissue. His introduction to the world in the town of Bethlehem was not the start of Him, since He generally was.

Every One of the Three-in-one God will be God. Every One has a specific work and each cooperates with the Others. What Christ resembled before the world was made is best found in John 17:5. "Presently, Father, respect Me with the respect I had with you before the world was made." And in John 17:24, "Father, I need My followers You offered Me to be with Me where I am.

At that point they may see My sparkling enormity which You gave Me since You cherished Me before the world was made." Man does not realize what that sparkling significance (Shining greatness) was.

At the point when Christ left all the significance and respect of paradise to go to the earth to live as a man among corrupt men - sinful men, He didn't set His enormity aside. He and the Father were One notwithstanding when He moved toward becoming as one who is owned by someone (John 14:7-11).

Philippians 2:6-7 says, "Jesus has dependably been as God may be. Be that as it may, He didn't hold to His rights as God. He set aside everything that had a place with Him and made Himself the same as a worker who is claimed by somebody. He wound up noticeably human by being conceived as a man."

CHAPTER
TWO

Christ Was Born A Man

The Holy scriptures show that Jehovah of the Old Testament moved toward becoming flesh in the individual of Jesus (The Christ) Who was conceived in the town of Bethlehem (Matthew 1:18-25; Luke 1:26-35; John 1:14; Acts 10:18; Romans 8:34;Galatians 4:4; I Timothy 3:16; Hebrews 2:14.).

The route Christ of heaven moved toward becoming substance on earth is told in Luke 1:34-35. This does not imply that men can see how it happened. Ephesians 3:19 says such things go past what can be caught on. Romans 11:33b says, "No man can comprehend His musings. Nobody can comprehend His ways."

Why Christ left paradise to come to earth in human tissue:

1. TO MAKE THE FATHER KNOWN. John 1:18. "The greatly cherished Son is next to the Father. No man has ever observed God. Be that as it may, Christ has made God known to us."
2. TO UNDERSTAND MAN. Hebrews 2:18. "Since Jesus was enticed as we are and

endured as we do, He comprehends us and He can help us when we are enticed."

3. TO TAKE AWAY SINS. I John 3:5. "You realize that Christ came to take away our transgressions. There is no transgression in Him."

4. TO SHOW MAN HOW TO LIVE. I Peter 2:21, "These things are every one of the a piece of the Christian life to which you have been called. Christ languished over us. This shows us we are to follow in His means."

5. TO DESTROY THE WORKS OF THE DEVIL. I John 3:8, "The individual who continues erring has a place with the fallen angel. The demon has trespassed from the earliest starting point. In any case, the Son of God came to decimate the works of the fallen angel.

6. TO WIN OVER DEATH. Jews 2:14, "the reality of the matter is that we share a similar Father with Jesus. Also, the reality of the matter is that we share a similar sort of fragile living creature and blood since Jesus turned into a man like us. He kicked the bucket as we should bite the dust. Through

His passing He wrecked the energy of the fallen angel who has the energy of death."

7. TO GET THINGS READY FOR HIS SECOND COMING. Jews 9:28, "It is the same with Christ. He gave Himself once to take away the transgressions of numerous. When He comes the second time, He won't have to give Himself again for wrongdoing. He will spare each one of the individuals who are sitting tight for Him."

Christs came into this world the same as every single other me BUT WITHOUT SIN. Since He was without wrongdoing (SIN), He could give Himself for man's transgression. Without wrongdoing, He could take the discipline for man's transgressions and set man free.

Christ Was True Man

He is genuine God and He is genuine man. When He ended up noticeably human substance, He not just turned into a human individual, He turned into a piece of the entire human family. However He was still of Three-in-one God in the meantime.

1. Christ is the Religious Leader Who made the path for man to go to God. Christ, without a doubt prepared for every one of us. Jews 7:23-28 says, "There must be numerous religious pioneers amid the season of the Old Way of Worship. They passed on and others needed to continue in their work. Be that as it may, Jesus lives for eternity. He is the Religious Leader until the end of time. It will never show signs of change.

Thus Jesus is capable, now and always, to spare from the discipline of transgression all who come to God through Him since He lives perpetually to appeal to God for them. We require a Religious Leader Who made the path for man to go to God. Jesus is blessed and has no blame. He has never trespassed and is unique in relation to corrupt men; He has the place of respect over the sky.

Christ dislike different religious pioneers. They needed to give endowments consistently on the altaar in love for their own particular sins first and after that for the wrongdoings of the general population. Christ did not need. He gave one present on the holy place and that blessing was Himself. It was done once and it was accomplished forever. The Law makes religious pioneers of men. These men are not great.

After the Law was given, God talked with a guarantee. He made His Son an impeccable Religious Leader until the end of time."

2. Christ will come back to earth once more. Acts 1:11 says, "They stated, "You men of the nation of Galilee, why do you stand turning upward into paradise? This same Jesus Who was taken from you into paradise will return similarly you saw Him go up into paradise."

Christ Is True God And True Man

Understand that Jesus Christ was both God and man in the meantime. He is known as the God-man. It mus be recalled that He was immaculate God and ideal man in one individual. He set aside everything that had a place with Him and He ended up plainly human by being conceived as a man, however not the slightest bit did He quit being God (Philippians 2:6-7; Colossians 2:9).

We read in John 1:1, "The Word (Christ) was before all else. The Word was with God. The

Word was "God." Here the Bible calls Jesus, God. Likewise in Hebrews 1:18 it says, "Yet about His Son, He says, 'O God, Your place of energy will keep going forever. Whatever You say in Your country is sright and great" (Genesis 1:26).

Christ, as God, is called God, the Son of God, Lord, King of Kings and Lord of Lords. He has all power, knows all, is all over the place, and does not change. He makes things, keep things going, excuses sins, offers life to the dead, and says who is liable. He is respected by holy messengers and men and one day all men will bow down before Him and say He is Lord.

Jesus left paradise and came to earth. Throough the capable work of God, Jesus was conceived in human substance. This is known as the virgin birth and it implies that the infant to be conceived came to be inside the mother without a father like other kids have. How was Jesus conceived? The introduction of Jesus Christ was this way: Mary His mom had been guaranteed in marriage to Joseph.

Before they were hitched, it was found out that she was to have an infant by the Holy Spirit" (Matthew 1:18). In Isaiah 7:14, some time before Jesus was conceived, it says, "So the Lord Himself will give you an extraordinary thing to see: A young lady, who had never had a man will bring forth a child. She will give Him the name Immanuel."

Matthew 1:20-23 says, "While he was pondering this, a heavenly attendant of the Lord came to him in a fantasy. The blessed messenger stated, "Joseph, son of David, don't be reluctant to take Mary as your better half. She is to end up plainly a mother by the Holy Spirit. A Son will be destined to her. You will give Him the name of Jesus since He will spare His kin from the discipline of their transgressions."

This Happened as the Lord said it would occur through the early evangelist. He stated, "The young lady, who has never had a man, will bring forth a Son. They will give Him the name Immanuel. This implies god with us (Isaiah 7:14). At the point when Jesus was conceived, He was conceived like any infant is conceived (Luke 2:6-7). In any case, how He came to be inside Mary was an extraordinary capable work of God by The Holy Spirit.

What was Mary, the Mother of Jesus like? In Luke 1:26-38 we read of a holy messenger disclosing to Mary that God had picked her from among numerous ladies to be the mother of Jesus by the Holy Spirit. She was picked as a result of the faith in God. Mary was a lady of respect (honor) to be the mother of Jesus, however she was not without wrongdoing. Jesus was conceived without transgression in light of the fact that the Holy Spirit was the One Who made Jesus come to be inside Mary.

It Is Important To Understand That Jesus Is The True God-Man

There are false teachers who say that He did not come in a human body (I John 4:2-3; 5:20-21). It is hard to understand how Christ was God and man at the same time. But in His life here on earth He was seen as both.

As a man He was tired, and yet as God He called the tired to Himself for rest.

As a man He was hungry, and yet as God He was "The Bread of Life."

As a man He was thirsty, and yet as God He was "The Water Of Life."

As a man He was in pain, and yet as God He healed those who were sick and in pain."

As a man He grew, and yet as God He was from the Beginning.

As a man He was tempted, and yet as God He could not be tempted.

As a man He did not know everything, and yet as a God He knew all things.

As a man He made Himself less important than the angels, and yet as God He was more important than they were.

As a man He said, "My Father is greater than I, and yet as God He said, "I and My Father are One."

As a man He prayed, and yet as God He answered prayer.

As a Man He cried at the grave, and yet as God He called the dead to arise.

As a man He died, and yet as God He is Life that last forever.

CHAPTER

THREE

Christ's Names And Meanings

There are more than 100 names given to Christ in God's Word. These names give Him respect and put Him high above everything. Everything that was, everything that is and everything that should happen, everything! Pass, present and future Christ's name is most importantly!

He is the Holy One, Lord of All, the Beginning and the End, He is God's Only Son, the Bright and Morning Star, and God's Greatest Gift. Christ is called Wonderful, The One Who goes along side to help, The Father that keeps going forever, the Prince of Peace. He is additionally the King of the Jews, the King of rulers, the Lord Strong and Powerful, the True God, and Lord capable to spare.

1. "Jesus" - This name intends to spare, to help, to make free. Matthew 1:21b says, ".... You will give Him the name of Jesus since He will spare His kin from the discipline of their wrongdoings.

2. "Christ" - The name Christ implies One Who was done "an uncommon employment

or Anointing One." It is the same as "Savior" in the Old Testament. "Blessing" intends to poor out oil on a man. In Old Testament times, men decided for an uncommon employment (undertaking) had oil poured over them. At first He was called "Jesus the Christ" yet later this was changed to "Jesus Christ." Matthew 16:16 says, "Simon Pert stated, "You are the Christ, the Son of the Living God."

3. "Ruler" - Lord implies that "He is Leader of the Church." John 9:38 says, "He stated, "I do put my trust in You, Lord." Then he got down before "Jesus" and worshiped Him."

4. "Child of Man" - This was a name "Jesus" called "Himself." It signifies "He was God," but then "He progressed toward becoming man. Luke 19:10 says, "For the Son of Man came to search for and to spare from the discipline of wrongdoing the individuals who are lost."

5. "Child of David" - This name implies that "God" was coming clean long prior when "He guaranteed Christ would come." Matthew 9:27 says, "Jesus" went ahead from that point. Two visually impaired men tailed

Him. They got out, Take feel sorry for on us, "Child of David" (Jeremiah 23:5).

6. "Immanuel" - This was the name give "Christ" when he was conceived. It signifies "God with us." Matthew 1:23b says, "....They will give Him the name Immanuel. This implies God with us (Isaiah 7:14).

He Is Also Called:

1. "The Word" - signifies "One" who helps men get it.
2. "Educator" - As instructor He instructed others.
3. "Religious Leader" - (High Priest) - He goes to "God" for man. On account of Adam all men were conceived in transgression, yet "Christ" made the route for men's wrongdoings to be excused.
4. "Sheep of God" - He was immaculate and the Only One Who could take away sins.

Many Names Tell Of The Work Christ Did:

1. The "Person Who" nurtures others, the One Who Saves, The Head Shepherd," and the

One Who bails us out of inconvenience or threat."

2. He is "Unwavering," "Genuine." "Companion of Sinners," "Endowment of God," the "Light of the World," and the "Person Who says what is correct or off-base."

3. He can be "trusted" in light of the fact that "He is the "Stone" and "Foundation," "the Way" and "the Door to paradise." "He" is "Life."

CHAPTER

FOUR

Christ's Death

The Old Testament told about the demise of Christ. In beginning 3:15 it says that Satan, the snake, would hurt the Special Person to come. Isaiah 53 tells about Christ putting men's wrongdoings on Himself. It demonstrates that the Special Person to come would bite the dust. Zechariah 13:6-7 says that the Shepherd would kick the bucket and the sheep would flee. In John 10 Jesus says that He is that Good Shepherd.

The Old Testament appeared in changed ways how Christ would bite the dust. Whenever Adam and Eve were put out of the garden of Eden, God made layers of skin for them which demonstrated that blood must be given to make a covering. Adam's child Abel slaughtered a sheep as a blessing on the holy place in love.

This was a photo of how Christ would bite the dust for men. This same picture was appeared in Exodus 12 where a sheep was murdered and the blood put on the entryway extraordinarily to demonstrate that transgressions were secured. In Numbers 21, when Moses made a snake from metal and put it up on a cross. Christ discussed that in John 3:14-15.

The New Testament shows that when Christ kicked the bucket, He passed on in the place of the individuals who had trespassed. I Peter 3:18 shows that Christ never trespassed yet God put men's wrongdoings on Him so men could be made appropriate with God. II Corinthians 5:21 shows that Christ let Himself be abhorred and rebuffed rather than man.

Galatians 3:13 shows that Christ passed on. Christ needed to kick the bucket as man bites the dust if He somehow happened to bite the dust in man's place for wrongdoing. But then His passing was arranged before God made the world and man. Despite the fact that He passed on, His demise was distinctive, Matthew 27:50 says, "Jesus ....gave up His Spirit and kicked the bucket." He needed to bite the dust for men and He was allowed to do as such.

At the point when the officers came to execute the men on the crosses, they didn't break Jesus' legs as they did the other two who were hanging alongside Him. They saw He was at that point dead, yet they slice His side no doubt. Whenever blood and water turned out, they were certain He was at that point dead.

Christ kicked the bucket to give His life for

men. He didn't pass on in light of the fact that the court said He should be slaughtered.

The nails did not hold Jesus on the cross. He gave His life for others that they may have life. Jews 10:10-14 says that He gave Himself as a blessing to God. Romans 5:6-9 says that He gave His life for all heathens and that His blood paid the discipline for transgression. I John 2:2 says that He paid for the transgressions of the entire world.

Since Jesus kicked the bucket, men can be spared. (Romans 5:9) Men can be spared or set free from the energy of wrongdoing over them. (John 8:32-36; Romans 6:10) Men can be spared from being liable of wrongdoing. (Romans 5:16-17). He spared men from the dread of wrongdoing (II Timothy 1:7). Christ spared men through adoration (John 4:9-10).

So His passing paid for the discipline of the transgressions of all men from Adam to the apocalypse. As Moses lifted up the snake in the Desert, so the Son of Man must be lifted up.

CHAPTER

FIVE

Christ Was Raised From The Dead

Reality that Jesus was raised froom the dead after He kicked the bucket on the cross to take the discipline for man's transgressions is a standout amongst the most essential truths in the Word of God. Being made ideal with God relies on upon this,

I Corinthians 15:17 says, "If Christ was not raised from the dead, your confidence merits nothing and you are as yet living in your transgressions." A man must trust that Christ was raised from the dead. It has been known for right around two-thousand years that Jesus was raised from the dead.

1. The Truth That Jesus Was Raised From The Dead Shows Numerous Things:
   A. It demonstrates that the Lord Jesus completed His work by biting the dust in man's place taking the discipline for his wrongdoing. God gotten Jesus' demise in our place.
   B. It demonstrates and guarantees to man that some time or another Christ will come back once more. Christ's passing on

the cross to take the discipline for man's wrongdoings would be of no utilization unless He had been raised from the dead (Romans 4:25; I Corinthians 15:14, 17). We realize that God got Christ's done work, since God raised Christ and placed Him in a position of energy at God's own correct side (Philippians 2:8-10; Hebrews 1:3).

On the off chance that Christ had not been raised from the dead, He couldn't have gone to Heaven. Furthermore, in the event that He had not gone to paradise, He couldn't return again to bring man to paradise with Him (I Thessalonians 4:14-16; Acts 1:3,9-11). However, He was raised from the dead!

C. Reality that Christ was raised from the dead is the most noteworthy truth of all circumstances (Acts 1:3). It is the best verification of the Christian method for love (Romans 1:4). It is the best show of God's energy (Ephesians 1:19- 20). It is the best truth of the Good News (I Corinthians 15:3-4; Romans 10:9-10). It is the best thing to make man accept and put stock in (I Thessalonians 4:14). It is the best thing to ensure man's coming pay for confiding in Christ (I Corinthians 15:20). It is the best thing to make man need to be heavenly (Romans 6:9-12).

D. Reality that Jesus was raised from the dead was so demonstrated to the adherents of Christ that they didn't have any uncertainty about it. They went out and lectured it without being perplexed. They lectured this even to individuals who abhorred them.

They were prepared to be executed for lecturing it. They told the individuals who were listening that they were blameworthy of murdering Jesus, the exceptionally One Whom God raised from the dead (Acts 2:23-24; 36b; 3:13-15). Those individuals were however furious they couldn't state that those things were not valid.

E. After His misery and passing, Jesus showed Himself alive to a hefty portion of His adherents. He was seen by them amid the 40 days He was on earth after He was raised from the dead. This is

confirmation that He was raised from
the dead.

He Showed Himself To Many People:

1. To 500 individuals who saw Him at one time
    (I Corinthians 15:6).
    1. To Mary Magdalene (John 20:14-16).
    2. To the ladies coming back from the tomb
        (Matthew 28:8- 10).
    3. To Peter (Luke 24:34).
    4. To His adherents toward night (Luke
        24:33-36).
    5. To the two adherents making progress
        toward Emmaus (Luke 24:13-31).
    6. To every one of the ministers eight days
        after the fact (John 20:26).
    7. To seven by the pool of Tiberias (John
        21:1-23).
    8. To James (I Corinthians 15:7).
    9. To the eleven (Matthew 28:16-20).
    10. To Stephen outside Jerusalem (Acts 7:55).
    11. To Paul close to the city of Damascus
        (Acts 9:3-6).
    12. In the House of God (Acts 22:17-21).

13. To John on the Island of Patmos (Revelation 1:10-19).

2. These Prove Jesus Was Raised From The Dead:

A. The vacant grave (Mark 16:5-6).

B. The grave garments had not been moved (Luke 24:12).

C. The way Christ acted in the wake of being raised fro the dead (Luke 24:36-40).

D. The early church showed it (Acts 13:29-31).

E. The changed existences of the devotees of Christ (Acts 13:47).

F. The changed from miscreant to Christian in Saul's life (Acts 9:1-180.

G. The New Testament demonstrates it.

H. The way Christ gives new life to a man demonstrates the more than whatever else.

3. The Truth That Jesus Was Raised From The Dead Was Talked About.

A. Quite a while back God demonstrated His kin what might occur later on.'

(1) The Old Testament tells about it (Job 19:25-26; Psalm 16:10).

(2) Christ Himself tells about it (Matthew17:22-23; 20:17-19).

(3) God finished what He guaranteed in the Holy Writings. (Acts 13:32a says, "We present to you the Good News about thePromise made to our fathers. God has completed this for us who are his youngsters. He did this by raising Jesus from the dead." Psalm 2:7b says, "You are My Son. Today I have turned into Your Father (Luke 24:45-46).

B. Blessed messengers and the individuals who loathed Him discussed it. Matthew 28:5-6 says, "The blessed messenger said to the ladies, "Don't be anxious,. I know you are searching for Jesus Who was nailed to the cross. He is not here! He has become alive once again as He said He would. Come and see where the Loaard lay (Matthew 28:11-15; Luke 24:1-4,7,23).

4. A portion Of The Things That Are Shown By Christ Being Raised From The Dead

A. It demonstrates that God the Father was cheerful to get Jesus.
B. It demonstrates that Jesus is God's Only (Unique) Son.
C. It indicates how Jesus can never be wrecked.
D. It indicates how Jesus has disarmed the demon and demise.
E. It indicates how the person who has put his trust in Christ is as though he had never trespassed.
F. It demonstrates the energy of Christ in the Christian.
G. It gives living would like to the Christian.
H. It gives the Christian a Religious Leader.
I. It guarantees the Christian that some time or another he as well, will be raised from the dead to be with God in paradise.
J. It demonstrates the world His truth.
K. It tells the world that all men will be raised up sometime in the not so distant future. They will be told they are blameworthy and will be rebuffed, or they will get their compensation for living for Christ.
L. It tells the world that sometime it will be let it know is liable.

Every other religion venerate a dead god. Christians are the main individuals who love a God who has prevailed upon death and lives today.

CHAPTER
SIX

Christ Was Taken Up To Heaven

1. Reality (The Truth) that Christ has been taken up into paradise and is at the right hand of the Father and has been given power and respect and enormity implies that God is satisfied with the work Christ did to take away our transgression (Hebrews 9).

2. Christ's Going to Heaven was required. The giving of power and honor and greatness to Christ was required.

   A. To complete His work to make men free (John 20:16-17).

   B. So his devotees could do more noteworthy works. John 14:12 says, "Without a doubt, I let you know, whoever puts his trust in Me can do the things I am doing. He will do much more noteworthy things than these on the grounds that I am setting off to the Father."

   C. So the Holy Spirit could be given. John 7:39 says, "Jesus said this in regards to the Holy Spirit Who might go to the individuals who put their trust in Him. The Holy Spirit had not yet been given.

Jesus had not yet been raised to the place of respect (John 16:7)."

D. So what He did could be known over all the world. Individuals over all the world could revere Him. Matthew 28:18-20 says, "Jesus came and said to them, "The sum total of what power had been given to Me in paradise and earth. Go and make supporters of the considerable number of countries.

Sanctify(Baptize) through water them for the sake of the Father and of the Son and of the Holy Spirit. Show them to do all things I have let you know. What's more, I am with you generally, even to the apocalypse."

E. So his supporters, both then and now, would have the capacity to advise others what happened to Jesus after He had passed on and had been raised from the dead. They saw Him taken up into paradise. Luke 24:50-51 says, :Jesus drove them out similar to Bethany.

The He lifted up His hands and asked that great would come to them. And keeping in mind that He was asking that great would come to them, He went from them was taken up to paradise and they worshiped Him" (Mark 16:9; Acts 1:9).

3. Christ's Work now is petitioning God for men as He sits at the correct side of God in Heaven. Jews 10:12b says, "Thus Jesus is capable, now and everlastingly, to spare from the discipline of wrongdoing all who come to God through Him since He lives always to appeal to God for them." (Isaiah 53:12b; Romans 8:26).

4. The Truth Of Christ being taken up into Heaven was instructed by:

   A. Peter- Acts 2:32-33 says, "Jesus is this One! God has raised Him up and we have all observed Him. This Jesus has been lifted up to God's correct side. The Holy Spirit was guaranteed by the Father. God has offered Him to us. That is the thing that you are seeing and hearing at this point!"

   B. Paul - Hebrews 8:1 says, "Now the vital thing is sthis. We have such a Religious Leader Who has made the route for man to go to God. He is the One Who sits at the correct side of the All-Powerful God in the sky (Ephesians 1:20-21;4:8-10)."

C. Stephen - Who saw Jesus at God's correct side. Acts 7:56 says, "He stated, "See! I see paradise open and the Son of Man remaining at the correct side of God!"

D. The Revelation Of Jesus Christ as given to John.

CHAPTER

SEVEN

Christ Received Great Honor

1. God's Word recounts Christ being raised from the dead and being brought up to be with the Father. He additionally was raised up to get significant privilege and was given a vital place.

    A. His supporters, remaining on the heap of Olives, saw Him go up (Luke 24:50-52). From that time on, they knew He had gone to be with the Father. At the supplication meeting as told in Acts 1, His adherents did not anticipate that Him will visit them as he had between the season of His being raised from the dead and heading off to the Father. They knew He was with the Father.

    B. Directly after He went to be with the Father, two blessed messengers disclosed to His supporters of His going. Acts 1:10-11 says, "They were all the while admiring paradise, watching Him go. At the same time two men wearing white remained next to them. They stated, "You men of the nation of Galilee, why do you stand gazing upward into paradise? This same Jesus Who was taken from you into paradise will return similarly you saw Him go up into paradise."

C. Peter lectured the many individuals the day the Holy Spirit went ahead the congregation, he recounted Christ being at the correct hand of God. Acts 2:33 says, "This Jesus had been lifted up to God's correct side. The Holy Spirit was guaranteed by the Father. God has offered Him to us. That is the thing that you are seeing and hearing at this point!"

D. Just before Stephen was murdered, he was permitted to investig*ate paradise, and he stated, "See! I see paradise open and the Son of Man remaining at the correct side of God!" (Acts 7:56)

E. Paul recounts this. Ephesians 1:20-21 says, "It is a similar power that raised Christ from the dead. This place was given to Christ. It is significantly more prominent than any ruler or pioneer can have. Nobody else can have this place of respect and power. Nobody in this world or on the planet to come can have such respect and power."

2. What happened when Christ was brought up to be with the Father.

   A. Christ rreturned to a similar place of sparkling significance He had before He cleared out. John 17:5 says, "Now Father, respect Me with the respect I had with You before the world was made (Hebrews 1:8-9; Revelation 5:11-12)."

   B. After Christ was reclaimed to paradise, the Holy Spirit descended upon the congregation. Jesus guaranteed this would happen, and it was one reason He came back to the Father. The Holy Spirit was not given until Christ had been raised to the place of respect. John 16:7 says, "I disclose to you reality. It is better for you that I leave. In the event that I don't go, the Helper won't come to you. On the off chance that I go, I will send Him to you."

   C. Another and living way has been opened to man which Christ made conceivable. Jews 10:20-21 says, "We now come to God by the new and living way. Christ made with along these lines for us. He opened the blind, which was His own body. We have an extraordinary Religious Leader over the place of God.

D. Since Christ was raised to the place of honor, man has seek after His arrival. Acts 2:20-21 says, "The sun will turn dim and the moon will swing to blood before the day of the Lord. His coming will be an extraordinary and exceptional day. It will be that whoever approaches the name of the Lord will be spared from the discipline of wrongdoing."

The first occasion when He came it was to deal with man's transgressions. The second time He comes He will take every one of the individuals who have put their trust in Him to be with Himself. Jews 9:28 says, "It is the same with Christ. He gave Himself once to take away the transgressions of numerous. When He comes the second time, He won't have to give Himself again for wrongdoing. He will spare each one of the individuals who are willing for Him."

It is from this high place of respect in paradise that Christ will come back once more. Philippians 3:20-21 says, "However we are residents of paradise (Heaven). Christ, the One who spares from the discipline of wrongdoing (sins), will descend from paradise once more. We are sitting tight for Him to return.

He will change these assemblages of our own of the earth and make them new. He will make them like His assemblage of sparkling significance. He has the ability to do this since He can make all things obey Him."

There were unique reasons Christ was brought up to be with the Father.

A. To offer respect to God. John 17:1 says, "When Jesus had said these things, He admired paradise and stated, "Father, the time has come! Respect Your Son so Your Son may respect you."

B. To make workable for men to put their trust in Him. I Timothy 3:16 says, "It is vital to know the mystery of God-like living, which is: Christ came to earth as a Man. He was unadulterated in His Spirit. He was seen by blessed messengers (angels). The countries found out about Him. Men wherever put their trust in Him. He was taken up into paradise."

C. To offer blessings to men. Ephesians 4:8 says, "The Holy Writings say, "When Christ went up to paradise, He took the individuals who were held with Him. He offered blessings to men.""

D. To give the endowment of the Holy Spirit. John 16:7 says, "I disclose to you reality. It is better for you that I leave. On the off chance that I don't go, the Helper won't come to you. On the off chance that I go, I will send Him to you."

E. To make a conclusion to the transgression issue. Jews 1:3 says, "The Son sparkles with the sparkling enormity of the Father. The Son is as God is all around. The Son holds up the entire world by the energy of His Word. The Son gave His own particular life so we could be spotless from all transgression. After He had done that, He sat down on the correct side of God in paradise."

F. So men may run with finish trust to the very place of God's adoring - support. Jews 4:14-16 says, "We have an awesome Religious Leader Who has made the path for man to go to God. He is Jesus, the Son of God, Who has gone to paradise to be with God. Give us a chance to keep our trust in Jesus Christ.

Our Religious Leader sees how feeble we are. Christ was enticed inside and out we are enticed, however He didn't sin. Release us with finish trust to the very place of God's cherishing - support. We will get his adoring - benevolence and have His cherishing - support to help us at whatever point we require it.

G. To make the route prepared for men to go to God. Jews 6:19-20 says, "This desire is a sheltered grapple for our souls. It will never move. This expectation goes into the Holiest Place of - All behind the window ornament of paradise. Jesus has effectively done there. He has turned into our Religious Leader perpetually and had made the route for man to go to God. He is Melchizedek (Genesis 14:18-20).

H. To spare from wrongdoing. Jews 7:25 says, "Thus Jesus is capable, now and perpetually, to spare from the discipline of transgression all who come to God through Him since He lives always to appeal to God for them." (Romans 8:34; Hebrews 9:24).

I. To be man's Religious Leader. Jews 8:1 says, "Now the vital thing is this: We have such a Religious Leader Who has made the route for man to go to God. He is the One Who sits at the correct side of the All-Powerful God in paradise."

J. To answer anything anybody says against Christians. Romans 8:33-34 says, "Who can state anything against the general population God has picked? It is God who says they are ideal with Himself. Who can then say we are liable? It was Christ Jesus Who passed on. He was raised from the dead. He is on the correct side of God appealing to Him for us."

K. To offer solace to men by their drawing close to God and clutching the expectation they have. Jews 10:22-23 says, "Thus let us drawing close to God with a genuine heart loaded with confidence. Our hearts must be made clean from liable sentiments and our bodies washed with immaculate water. Give us a chance to clutch the expectation we say we have and not be changed. We can trust God that He will do what He guaranteed."

L. To make it workable for us to do more noteworthy things. John 14:12 says, "Without a doubt, I let you know, whoever put his trust in Me can do the things I am doing. He will do significantly more noteworthy things that these in light of the fact that I am heading off to the Father.

M. To give men a place with Christ in the sky. Ephesians 2:6 says, "God raised us up from death when He raised up Christ Jesus. he has given us a place with Christ in the sky." (John 14:1-3)

N. To give Jesus a name that is more noteworthy than whatever other name, so that everybody will offer respect to God the Father. Philippians 2:8-9 says, "After He turned into a man, He surrendered His vital place and obeyed by biting the dust on a cross. Along these lines, God lifted Jesus high above everything else. He gave Him a name that is more noteworthy than any othere name."

O. To fill all the world with Himself. Ephesians 4:10 says, "Christ Who went down into the profound additionally went up far over the sky. He did this to fill all the world with Himself."

P. So Christ may have the ability to run the show. Matthew 28:18 says, "Jesus came and said to them, 'The sum total of what power had been given to Me in paradise and earth." (Acts 3:20-21; Hebrews 10:12-13; I Peter 3:22).

Q. So Christ could assume His correct position as leader of the congregation. Colossians 1:18 says, "Christ is the leader of the congregation which is His body. He is the start for goodness' sake. He is the first to be raised from the dead. He is to have ahead of all comers in everything." (Ephesians 4:15-16; 5:30-32).

R. To clean the sky where Satan conflicted with God. In Hebrews 9:23-24 it says that the blood of creatures was utilized to clean the place of God which was a photo of the place of God in paradise. Be that as it may, paradise required an option that is superior to the blood of creatures. It needed to have the blood of Christ.

CHAPTER
EIGHT

Christ Spoke For God

In Deuteronomy 18:18-19 it says, "I will give them a man who represents God like you from among their siblings. I will put MY words in his mouth. What's more, he will make known to them all that I let him know. He will talk in my name. What's more, I will rebuff whoever won't hear him out." Long back one of the early ministers said that Christ would be One Who represented God. (Acts 3:22).

The first and most essential importance of "prophet" is one who conveys things to light. It likewise implies one who tells what will happen. In the Old Testament the name implied: one who sees, or one who sees what the eye does not see. The "New Testament significance is," one who addressed the general population must talk what God needed talked. The significance in both Old and New Testaments demonstrate that "Christ was One Who Spoke For God."

1. Early Preachers Spoke For God.

Many imagine that a prophet is one who advises just what will occur later on. This is "Not True." The One who represented God amid the season of Israel was keen on "what was going on too" as "what would occur later on." Much of what the individuals who represented God said to the general population was in regards to what was going on then.

However, they additionally said numerous things that needed to do with what's to come. God utilized uncommon men He picked in Old Testament times to address His kin, however He utilized Christ to address His kin in the seasons of the New Testament.

Jews 1:1-2a says, "Long back God addressed our initial fathers in a wide range of ways. He talked through the early evangelists. Be that as it may, in these last days He has addressed us through His child."

2. Christ Spoke For God.

Christ was One Who represented God from the time He was sanctified through water at the Jordan River until He was nailed to the cross on Calvary. Acts 2:22 says, "Jewish men, tune in to what I need to state! You knew Jesus of the town of Nazareth by the effective works He did. God worked through Jesus while He was with you. All of you know this." (Matthew 4:23-25; Luke 4:14-17; Hebrews 9:26-28).

Amid the time He was on earth, Christ represented God about vital things later on.

A. He discussed His passing and about His being raised from the dead (Matthew 12:39-40; 26:1-2; John 2:19-22).

B. He told what might occur between the season of His passing and the time Jerusalem would be devastated (Matthew 24:4-14; Mark 13:13; Luke 21:5-24).

C. He told that Jerusalem would be devastated, and that the Christians would endure and be executed and be sent all over. Additionally He told about an exceptionally corrupt man-made god that would remain in the place of God in Jerusalem (Matthew 24:15-22; Mark 13:14-23; Luke 21:20-28).

D. He told that the Good News would be lectured over all the earth (Matthew 24:14).

E. He advised how He would come back again to earth (See Chapter on Christ's Second Coming).

3. In the past there have been "false evangelists," and there are some today. Certain tests appear in the event that they are "false ministers."

   A. Christ gave a test that can be utilized today. "So you will know them by their organic product" (Matthew 7:20). They attempt to demonstrate they are ones who represent God by doing effective things, however they are false.

   B. On the off chance that early evangelists did not lecture against transgression and advise men to be sad for their wrongdoing and turn from it, they were false. it is a similar today.

   C. False evangelists can be tried by the Word of God. Regardless of the possibility that they do a wide range of things that look like intense works, if what they say is not consistent with what the Word of God says, they are false.

   D. The spirits can be tried. I John 4:13 says, "Dear Christian companions, don't trust each soul. In any case, test the spirits to check whether they are from God for there are numerous false ministers on the planet. You can tell if the soul is from

God along these lines: Every soul says Jesus Christ has arrived in a human body is from God.

Furthermore, every soul that does not state Jesus has arrived in a human body is not from God. It is the instructing of the false christ. You have heard that this educating is coming. It is now here on the planet.

CHAPTER

NINE

CHAPTER
NINE

Christ: Man's Religious Leader

A religious pioneer is one who remains amongst God and man, and goes to the ideal God for the liable delinquent. The Word of God tells that Christ is our "Religious Leader." Hebrews 5:6; 6:20 say, "God says in another piece of His Word, "You will be a Religious Leader until the end of time. You will resemble Melchizedek.""

"Jesus has officially done there. He has turned into our Religious Leader perpetually and has made the route for man to go to God. He resembles Melchizedek (Psalm 110:4)."

1. Christ was all things a religious pioneer must be.

   A. In the Old Way of Worship there were exceptional religious pioneers for the Jewish individuals. These men were called ministers and they were aides remaining amongst God and man. In Hebrews 5:1-4 it advises what a religious pioneer must be:

      (1) He was browsed among men (Hebrews 5:4-6).

(2) He was a partner remaining amongst God and man.

(3) He gave endowments from the general population on the sacrificial stone to love to God.

(4) He gave blood from creatures for the transgressions of the general population.

(5) A Jewish religious pioneer was only a man himself and powerless from numerous points of view. What's more, since he was frail he needed to offer endowments to God for his own particular sins and in addition for the transgressions of the general population.

(6) God picked the man for his work.

(7) Under the Jewish Law, Levi and his children were the religious pioneers, and every single religious pioneer were to get through that family (Hebrews 7:11).

B. Jesus Christ is man's Religious Leader! It is He Who has made the route for man to go to God. Christ could be man's Religious Leader on the grounds that:

(1) He was looked over among men (Hebrews 5:4-6).

(2) He was more than an aide remaining amongst God and men. He is man's Religious Leader Who made the path for him to go to God.

(3) Christ gave just a single blessing on the sacred place and that was Himself. He was an immaculate blessing and never again does a blessing need to be given for man's wrongdoings (Hebrews 9:25-26).

(4) Christ gave His own blood, not the blood of creatures like alternate religious pioneers did.

(5) Jesus Christ, man's Religious Leader, is blessed and has no blame. He has never trespassed and is not quite the same as evil men (Hebrews 7:26). That is the reason He could give Himself as a present for all men and not need to give one for Himself like alternate religious pioneers did.

(6) God picked Christ to be man's Religious Leader (Hebrews 5:6).

(7) Jesus did not originate from the group of Levi but rather from the group of Judah. Those from the group of Levi were not ready to give endowments which would keep going always on the sacred place for the wrongdoings of the general population. God changed this. Jesus was from another family, and He was the Gift which was impeccable all around. He then could be given for the transgressions of the general population (Hebrews 7:11-14).

2. Christ did all things a religious pioneer needed to do.

A. In the Old Way of Worship the religious pioneer did three unique things:

(1) He murdered creatures and gave them on the sacred place as a blessing in love for the general population.

(2) He went inside the Holy Place to petition God for the general population. The head religious pioneer went into the Holiest Place of All once every year taking the blood of a

creature to give for his own particular sins and for the transgressions of the considerable number of individuals (Hebrews 9:6-7).

(3) After he gave the blood in the Holiest Place of All, he turned out. At that point he expressed gratefulness and supplicated that great would go to the general population.

B. As Our awesome Religious Leader, Christ did each of the three things:

  (a) He gave Himself as a blessing on the sacrificial table. Jews 9:14 says, "The amount increasingly the blood of Christ will do! He gave Himself as an ideal blessing to God through the Spirit that lives for eternity. Presently your heart can be free from the blameworthy work for the living God."

  (b) Christ is currently going to God for man. Romans 8:334 says, "Who then can state we are blameworthy? It was Christ Jesus Who passed on. He was raised from the dead. He is on the correct side of God petitioning Him for us.

"Jews 7:25 says, "Thus Jesus is capable, now and everlastingly, to spare from the discipline of transgression all who come to God through Him since He lives perpetually to appeal to God for them."

> (c) At the point when Christ comes to earth the second time, He will bring with Him each one of the individuals who have put their trust in Him. Jews 9:28 says, "It is the same with Christ. He gave Himself once to take away the wrongdoings of numerous. When He comes the second time He won't have to give Himself again for transgression. He will spare each one of the individuals who are sitting tight for Him (I Thessalonians 4:16; I Peter 1:5; Revelation 20:4).

Jews 4:15-16 says, "Our Religious Leader sees how feeble we are. Christ was enticed inside and out we are enticed, however He didn't sin. Release us with finish trust to the very place of God's cherishing support. We will get His cherishing thoughtfulness and have His adoring support to help us at whatever point we require it."

CHAPTER

TEN

Christ's Death In Man's Place

"Atonement" implies the work of Christ when He offered Himself to pay for the transgressions of liable miscreants to fulfill God Who, being heavenly, detests sin. This was finished by Christ's blessed life, His demise on the cross set up of the miscreant. His being raised from the dead, and His accepting significant privilege in paradise.

"Atonement" is not found in many interpretations of the Bible, but rather it is frequently utilized when talking about the work of Christ. God gave what was expected to make peace between the heathen and Himself. Man did not make a way, God dealt with it for man. Man would never work his way up to God. God came down to man to deal with his need.

1. The Teaching Of Christ's Death In Our Place Is Important Both In Heaven And On Earth.
   A. It is something the blessed messengers needed to think about. I Peter 1:11-12 says, "The early ministers marveled at what time or to what individual this would happen. The Spirit of Christ in

them was conversing with them and educated them to compose regarding how Christ would endure and about His sparkling significance later on.

They knew these would not occur amid the time they lived but rather while you are living numerous years after the fact. These are the very things that were advised to you by the individuals who lectured the Good News. The Holy Spirit Who was sent from paradise gave them power and they recounted things that even the heavenly attendants might want to think about.

B. Christ Himself ssaid this was the most essential piece of His work. Stamp 10:45 says, "For the Son of Man did not come to be watched over. He came to tend to others. He came to give His life so that many could be purchased by His blood and be made free from wrongdoing."

C. Christ knew this instructing would draw in men to Him. John 12:32 says, "And when I am lifted up from the earth, I will pull in all individuals toward me."

D. The Holy Writings (Scriptures) educate much concerning Christ giving Himself for heathens. The passing of Christ is talked about more than 175 times in the New Testament. Paul discusses it frequently, as do other New Testament essayists.

God's adoring - support to man implies love in real life. Indeed, even before man realized what his need was, God dealt with it. Romans 4:25; 5:6 say, "Jesus kicked the bucket for our transgressions. He was raised from the dead to make us ideal with God." "We were powerless and couldn't help ourselves. At that point Christ came at the correct time and gave His life for all miscreants."

There are numerous religions that advise men they can go to God after they turn out to be great. This is NOT TRUE. God's Word says that He makes men know they are miscreants and gives them a craving to be free from transgression.

Bogus methods for love attempt to take men to God. Be that as it may, men, being delinquents, are not prepared to remain before God. The genuine method for love is conceivable in light of the fact that God moved toward becoming man, and in doing as such, He made the path for men to go to Himself.

2. Four Reasons Why Christ Had To Die In Man's Place.
   A. God is sacred. At the point when man initially trespassed, this was not satisfying to God. God, being sacred, detests sin. In any case, God is not just sacred, He is likewise cherish. He cherished man, not on account of man had no transgression, but rather while man was a delinquent. Romans 5:8 says, "However God demonstrated His affection to us. While we were yet miscreants, Christ kicked the bucket for us."

Regardless of the possibility that a heathen quit doing awful things, it would change his wishes and musings. The heathen would at present be at war with God. God is sacred and He can not overlook these things. He can't love the transgression, yet He loves the delinquent.

The response to this issue was in the passing of Christ, God's own Son. Christ took upon

Himself the discipline that ought to have been given to the heathen. Since God is heavenly, something must be finished. His Son made a move. He kicked the bucket in our place.

B. The Laws of God were broken so a blessing must be given to God. Just an impeccable blessing could be given on the holy place in love. Christ was that Perfect Gift. He is the special case Who could be a blessing on the holy place for the miscreant.

C. At the point when a man sins, his heart reveals to him that he is liable. Peace and rest can't come until the delinquent realizes that his transgression is pardoned. At the point when the miscreant realize that Christ took his discipline upon Himself, peace and rest come to him. Romans 5:1 says, "Now that we have been made ideal with God by putting our trust in Him, we have tranquility with Him. It is a result of what our Lord Jesus Christ accomplished for us."

D. The lost miscreant knows he is lost. His heart discloses to him that he is blameworthy. At the point when the Holy

Spirit addresses him through the Word of God, he perceives the amount he has infringed upon God's Law, and how lost he is. On the off chance that man is to be spared from wrongdoing, the One Who never trespassed must discover him and spare him. This is exactly what Christ did. Luke 19:10 says, "For the Son of Man came to search for and to spare from the discipline of transgression the individuals who are lost."

3. What Christ Did When He Died In Our Place Was Important Because:

A. It was the most essential explanation behind Christ being conceived (Matthew 1:21).

B. It has an essential place in the initial four books of the New Testament. Each of the four authors of these books told numerous things. Be that as it may, with extraordinary think they told about the life and demise of Christ. Of the twenty-one parts in the book of John, ten of them recount the things prompting Christ's demise and of His being raised from the dead.

C. Christ came to earth to demonstrate that what God had guaranteed to the early fathers was valid. Through the Old Way of Worship, God at various circumstances had guaranteed to send His Son into the world (Romans 15:8; II Timothy 1:9; II Peter 1:10-12).

D. Christ turned into a man so He could make His Father known. "No man has ever observed God. Be that as it may, Christ has made God known to us" (John 1:18b). Jesus showed us numerous things about God the Father. He showed us that God the Father cherishes us. John 16:27 says, "....because the Father love you. He adores you since you cherish Me and trust that I originated from the Father.

E. Christ came to be the Religious Leader Who made the path for man to go to God. In the book of Hebrews it shows us that the head Jewish religious pioneers were taken from among men with the goal that they would act in the place of men. (Jews 5:1-2) In Hebrews 5:4-5 it additionally reveals to us that similarly, Christ was taken from among men so He could act in the place of men before God.

Jews 2:17-18 says, "So Jesus needed to wind up noticeably like His siblings inside and out. He must be one of us to be our Religious Leader to go amongst God and us. He had adoring compassion on us and He was reliable. He gave Himself as a blessing to pass on a cross for our transgressions with the goal that God would not hold these wrongdoings against us any more. Since Jesus was enticed as we are and endured as we do, He comprehends us and He can help us when we are enticed."

I Corinthians 10:13 says, "You have never been enticed to sin in any unique route than other individuals. God is dependable. He won't enable you to be enticed more than you can take. In any case, when you are enticed, He will make a route for you to keep from falling into transgression."

F. Christ kicked the bucket with the goal that He could pulverize sin. "He offered Himself to wreck sin" (Hebrews 9:26b). (Check 10:45b; John 3-5; II Corinthians 5:21; Romans 5:21; 6:12-18; Hebrews 2:8).

G. Christ passed on to devastate the works of the fallen angel. "Be that as it may, the Son of God came to demolish the works of the villain" (I John 3:8b), (John 12:31; Hebrews 2:14-15;Revelation 20:10a).

H. Christ kicked the bucket to make prepared for the time He will come back once more. "....when he comes the second time, He won't have to give Himself again for wrongdoing" (Hebrews 9:28). (Romans 8:18-25; Revelation 21:27).

I. Christ kicked the bucket so the individuals who have put their trust in Him may have life, "an extraordinary full life." (John 10:10b; Romans 5:1; 8:1-3; Hebrews 2:14-15; I John 4:10).

4. Who Did Christ Die For? I Timothy 2:6 - "He gave His life for all men so they could go free and not be held by the energy of sin...." Hebrews 2:9 says, "However we do see Jesus. For a little time He had a spot that was not as imperative as the heavenly attendants. However, God had adoring - support for everybody. He had Jesus endure passing on a cross, for every one of us.

At that point, in light of Christ's passing on a cross, God gave Him the prize of respect and sparkling significance." I John 2:2 says, "He paid for our wrongdoings with His own blood. He didn't pay for our own, however for the wrongdoings of the entire world."

Be that as it may, the reparation is great just for the individuals who take God's Gift. God cherishes all delinquents, yet just the individuals who put their trust in Him will be spared from wrongdoing. Romans 10:9 - "On the off chance that you say with your mouth that Jesus is Lord, and have confidence in your heart that God raised Him from the dead, you will be spared from the discipline of wrongdoing."

Christ isolated time. All things before Christ were finished anticipating Christ's introduction to the world. Every one of the things that occurred after Christ's demise think back to what He did when he kicked the bucket on the cross. Christ stated, "Nobody can have more prominent love than to give his life for his companions" (John 15:13). Men have given their lives for their companions, yet Christ had extraordinary love for the individuals who were not even his friends.''Romans 5:8: "yet God demonstrated His affection to us.

While we were yet delinquents, Christ passed on for us." He originated from paradise to the cross and bowed His head in a demise of disgrace and agony. His was the best blessing that was given to men. "For God so cherished the world that He gave His exclusive Son. Whoever puts his trust in God's Son won't be lost, yet will have life that keeps going forever" (John 3:16).

CHAPTER

ELEVEN

There Is Something Man Must Do

Man knows he is wrong with God. He know he is a delinquent and is lost. There is nothing man can do in his own particular energy to wind up noticeably appropriate with God.

1. Man Must Believe There Is A God

In Hebrews 11:6 it says, "Any individual who comes to God must trust that He is...." When a man trusts, he is certain of a truth and acknowledges it as truth. It is critical that he trusts God is, as well as that he trusts Christ kicked the bucket to spare delinquents, and was raised up from the grave to be the living One Who spares from the discipline of wrongdoing (Isaiah 53::1-12; I Corinthians 15:3-4).

However, trusting, alone, is insufficient. In James 2:19: "You accept there is one God. That is great! In any case, even the evil presences trust that, and in light of the fact that they do, they shake." The devils of Satan accept (as it were, they know reality and acknowledge it as truth) yet they do close to accept.

2. Man Must Have Faith In God

Jews 11:6a: "A man can't please God unless he has confidence." Hebrews 11:1 reveals to us what confidence is. "Presently confidence is the being certain we will get what we seek after. It is in effect beyond any doubt of what we can't see." If a man just trusts that there is a God, however does not have confidence in Him, then HE IS NOT SAVED FROM THE PUNISHMENT OF HIS SIN.

3. Man Must Trust Christ To Save Him From Sin.

Trust is the activity that accompanies accepting and confidence. Trust is not quite the same as accepting or confidence. This trust intends to put one's self into the care of the One in Whom he has confidence.

4. Man Must Be Sorry For His Sins And Turn From Them.

This is called "Contrition!" Repentance is a change of one's heart and mind that will prompt an adjustment in what he will do.

1. It is conceivable to feel sorry in view of transgression (sin), but then want to stop. The rich man in hellfire shouted out for cherishing graciousness. He was loaded with distress however it was past the point where it is possible to be sad for his wrongdoings and turn from them (sins).

Luke 16:24-28 says, "He shouted out and stated, "Father, Abraham, show compassion for me. Send Lazarus. Give him a chance to put the finish of his finger in water and cool my tongue. I am in much torment in this fire. Abraham stated, "My child, bear in mind that when you were living you had your great things.

Lazarus had terrible things. Presently he is all around tended to. You are in torment. What's more, more than this, there is a major profound place between us. Nobody from here can go there regardless of the possibility that he needed to go. Nobody can originate from that point. At that point the rich man stated, "Father, then I implore you to send Lazarus to my dad's home. I have five siblings. Give him a chance to let them know of these things, or they will result in these present circumstances place of much agony moreover."

The individuals who are not heartbroken for their wrongdoings now and won't turn from them will some time or another cry and granulate their teeth. They will have distress, however it is currently the same as being sad at this point.

5. Man Must Tell His Sins To God, And Tell Of God To Other Men.

   A. To God - God needs man to advise his wrongdoings to Him so He can pardon him. I John 1:9 says, "On the off chance that we disclose to Him our transgressions, He is loyal and we can rely on upon Him to excuse our wrongdoings. He will make our lives clean from all transgression."

   B. To men - Men who have placed their in Christ as the One Who spares must tell other men what has been done in their lives. Romans 10:10b says, ".....We tell with our mouth how we were spared from the discipline (punishment) of wrongdoing (sin).

CHAPTER
TWELVE

What God Does

There Are Some Things That Happen When A Man Puts His
Confidence In Christ....

1. He Becomes A New Person
   II Corinthians 5:17 - "For if a man has a place with Christ, he is another individual. The old life is no more. New life has started."

2. He Is Given A New Life
   Titus 3:4-5 - "Yet God, the One Who spares, demonstrated how lord He was and how He cherished us by sparing us from the discipline of transgression. It was not on account of we attempted to be ideal with God. It was a direct result of His adoring - thoughtfulness that He washed our transgressions away. In the meantime He gave us new life when the Holy Spirit came into our lives."

3. He is Made Right With God
   Romans 3:24 - "Anybody can be made appropriate with God by the unconditional present of His adoring - support. It is Jesus Christ Who got them with His blood and made

them free from their wrongdoings." (Romans 4:24).

4. He Is Saved From The Punishment Of Sin, And It's Guilt And Blame.

Romans 5:9 - "Now that we have been spared from the discipline of wrongdoing by the blood of Christ, He will spare us from God's outrage moreover." (Ephesians 2:5,8).

5. He Is Bought And Made Free From Sin.

Ephesians 1:7 - "In light of the blood of Christ, we are purchased and made free from the discipline of wrongdoing. What's more, due to His blood, our wrongdoings are excused. His adoring - support to us is so rich." (I Peter 1:19).

6. He Is In God's Family.

Ephesians 2:19 - "Starting now and into the foreseeable future you are not outsiders and individuals who are not subjects.

You are nationals together with the individuals who have a place with God. You have a place in God's family."

(Romans 8:15,23; 9:4; II Corinthians

6:17-18; Galatians 3:26; 4:4-7; Ephesians 1:4-11; I John 3:2).

7. He Is Baptized Into The Body Of Christ By The Holy Spirit.

I Corinthians 12:13 - "It is a similar path with us. Jews or the individuals who are not Jews, men who are possessed by somebody or men who are allowed to would what they like to do, have all been sanctified through water into the one body by a similar Holy Spirit. We have all gotten the one Spirit."

8. He Is Part Of God's Building.

Ephesians 2:22 - "You are likewise being assembled as a piece of this building since God lives in you by His Spirit."

9. He Is Given A Place With Christ In Heaven.

Ephesians 2:6 - "God raised us up from death when He raised up Christ Jesus. He has given us a place with Christ in the sky."

10. He Is Marked For God By The Holy Spirit.

Ephesians 1:13 - "The fact of the matter is the Good News. When you heard reality, you put your trust in Christ. At that point God stamped you by giving you His Holy Spirit as a guarantee."

11. He Is Set Apart For God - Like Living.

I Corinthians 6:11 - "Some of you were that way. Be that as it may, now your transgressions are washed away. You were separate for God-like living to do His work. You were made appropriate with God through our Lord Jesus Christ by the Spirit of God."

12. He Receives Gifts From The Holy Spirit.

I Corinthians 12:4-11 - "There are various types of blessings. Yet, it is a similar Holy Spirit Who gives them.

There are various types of work to be accomplished for Him. Be that as it may, the work is for a similar Lord. There are distinctive methods for doing His work. Yet, it is a similar God who utilizes all these courses in all individuals.

The Holy Spirit works in every individual in somehow for the benefit of all of us. One individual is given the endowment of showing useful tidbits. Someone else is given the endowment of educating what he has realized and knows. These blessings are by a similar Holy Spirit.

One Person gets the endowment of confidence. Another gets the blessings of recuperating. Propositions endowments are given by a similar Holy Spirit. One individual is given the endowment of speaking God's Word. Someone else is given the endowment of talking in exceptional sounds. Someone else is given the endowment of telling what these exceptional sounds mean. However, it is a similar Holy Spirit, the Spirit of God, who does every one of these things. He provides for every individual as He needs to give." (Romans 12:5-8; Ephesians 4:11-12).

CHAPTER
THIRTEEN

Christ's Second Coming

It tells all through God's Word that "Christ" will come to earth once more. Before Christ came to earth the first run through, the early ministers told about it in a considerable lot of the books of the Old Testament. In the initial four books of the New Testament it recounts how Christ came to earth. It was all similarly as the early pioneers had composed (early ministers).

Similar righteous men expounded on how Christ will come to earth the second time. We have no motivation to trust He won't come similarly as they told about it long prior.

1. The Bible Speaks Of Christ's Second Coming.

It recounts His second coming eight times more regularly than of His initially coming. It discusses it 318 times in The New Testament.

2. Church Leaders Taught That Christ Would Return.

Acts 3:20 - "He will send Jesus back to the world. He is the Christ Who long prior was decided for you." II Thessalonians 1:7 - "He will help you and us who are enduring." "This will happen when the Lord Jesus descends from paradise with His effective holy messengers in a splendid fire" (James 5:8; II Peter 1:16; I John 2:28; Jude 14).

3. The Angels Told Of Christ's Return.

Acts 1:11 - "They stated, You men of the coountry of Galilee, why do you stand gazing upward into paradise? This same Jesus Who was taken from you into paradise will return similarly you saw Him go up into paradise."

4. Jesus Told Of His Return.

Matthew 24:27 - "The Son of Man will come as quick as lightning goes over the sky from east to west." (Mark 13:26; Luke 21:27; John 14:3; 21:22).

The second happening to Christ is exactly what it says it is in plain dialect. Christ Himself is coming back again as a man and will be seen by everybody. Disclosure 1:7 - "See! He is coming in the mists.

Each eye will see Him. Indeed, even the men who executed Him will see Him. Every one of the general population on earth will shout out in distress as a result of Him."

A portion of the Old Testament early ministers composed of Christ's first and second coming without recounting the numerous years in the middle. At the point when a man takes a gander at two mountains that are far off, he doesn't see the valley between them. They look to him as though they are near one another.

Christ's Second Coming Will Be At Two Different Times

1. FOR THE CHRISTIANS (THE RAPTURE!!!)

The first run through Christ comes later on, He will desire the Christians. Amid the first occasion when He will come noticeable all around (sky) and the Christians will meet him there. My Brothers and My Sisters in Christ, I need you to know without a doubt about the individuals who have kicked the bucket. You have no motivation to be miserable or troubled as the individuals who have no expectation.

We trust that Jesus kicked the bucket and afterward returned to life once more. Since we trust this, we realize that God will enliven "every one of" the individuals who have a place with Jesus. We disclose to you this as it originated from the Lord. Those of us who are alive when the Lord comes back again won't venture out in front of the individuals who have kicked the bucket. For the Lord Himself will descend from paradise with a noisy call. The head holy messenger will talk with a noisy voice. God's horn will give its sounds.

To begin with, the individuals who have a place with Christ will leave their graves to meet the Lord. At that point, those of us who are as yet living here on earth will be assembled with them in the mists. We will meet the Lord in the sky and be with Him until the end of time. Along these lines, comfort each other with these words.

2. WITH THE CHRISTIANS (REVELATION!!!)

The second time Christ comes later on, He will accompany the Christians. Amid this second time He will go to the earth where He and the Church will run the countries. This is known as the "Disclosure." In Zechariah 14:4 - "On that day His feet will remain on the Mount of Olives, before Jerusalem on the east. Also, the Mount of Olives will be separated in two from east to west by a substantial valley.

Half of the mountain will advance toward the north and the other half toward the south."

THE GREAT TIME OF TROUBLE!!!

1. There will be seven years of particularly inconvenience on earth. This is known as the "Incomparable Tribulation."

Places of worship are separated regarding what they accept about when Christ will restore the first run through.

    A. "Pre-tribulation" implies that Christ will return before the seven years of much inconvenience.

    B. "Mid-tribulation" implies that Christ will return amidst the seven years, or following three and one-half years of much inconvenience.

    C. "Post-tribulation" implies that Christ will return after the seven years of much inconvenience.

CHAPTER
FOURTEEN

Signs Of The Times

Certain things demonstrate that Christ's arrival is sooner rather than later. Luke 21:31 - "similarly, when you see these things happening, you will know the sacred country of God is close to." The Word of God discloses to us that we ought to think about these things so we won't be astonished (I Thessalonians 5:1-4).

However, we can't know the day or the hour. Just God realizes that. Matthew 24:36 - "Yet nobody knows the day or the hour." No! Not even the holy messengers in paradise know. The Son does not know. Just The Father knows."

The Signs Are Given
(Matthew 24:3-14)

1. Many individuals will utilize Christ's name falsy. Verse 5 - "I am Christ." They will trick many individuals and will swing them to the wrong way."
2. There will be wars and bunches of discuss wars. Verses 6-7a - "You will know about wars and loads of discuss wars, yet don't be perplexed. These things must happen, yet it

is not the end yet. Countries will have wars with different countries. Nations will battle against nations.

3. There will be no nourishment for individuals. Verse 7b - "There will be no sustenance for individuals."

4. The Earth will shake and break separated in better places. Verse 7c - "The earth will shake and break separated in better places.

5. Christians will be harmed and slaughtered and despised. Verse 9 - "Then they will hand you over to be harmed. They will slaughter you. You will be abhorred by all the world on account of "MY NAME."

6. Many individuals will surrender and dismiss. Verse 10 - "Many individuals will surrender and dismiss as of now. Individuals will hand over each other. They will loathe each other.

7. Numerous false prophets, religious educators will begin working. Verse 11 - "Numerous false religious instructors will come. They will trick many individuals and will swing them to the wrong way.

8. Due to individuals violating the laws and sin being all over the place, The affection in the hearts of many individuals will wind

up plainly cool. Verses 12-13: "In light of individuals violating the laws and sin being all over the place, the affection in the hearts of many individuals will end up plainly frosty. Be that as it may, the person who remains consistent with the end will be spared."

These Signs Are Also Given:

9. There will be significantly more sin, yet individuals will state all is well and safe. I Thessalonians 5:3 - "When they say, 'All is well and safe,' then at the same time they will be wrecked. It will resemble torment that goes ahead a lady when a tyke is conceived. They won't have the capacity to make tracks in an opposite direction from it."

10. Individuals will love themselves and Money. II Timothy 3:2a - "Individuals will love themselves and cash. They will have pride and recount every one of the things they have done. They will talk against God."

11. Kids and youngsters won't comply with their folks. II Timothy 3:2b - "Youngsters and youngsters won't comply with their folks."

12. Individuals won't be grateful and they won't be blessed. II Timothy 3:2c: "Individuals won't be appreciative and they won't be blessed."

13. Individuals won't love each other. They will love fun as opposed to adoring God. II Timothy 3:3-4: "They won't love each other. Nobody can coexist with them. They will enlighten lies concerning others. They won't have the capacity to keep from doing things they know they ought not do.

They will be wild and need to beat and hurt the individuals who are great. They won't remain consistent with their companions. They will act without considering. They will think excessively of themselves. They will love fun as opposed to cherishing God.

14. The Jews will come back to their country. Ezekiel 36:24 - "For I will take you from the countries and accumulate you from every one of the terrains, and bring you into your own territory."

15. The Good News of Christ will be lectured everywhere throughout the world. Matthew 24:14 - "This Good News about the sacred country of God must be lectured over all the

earth. It must be advised to all countries and afterward the end will come."

16. The Jews will make the waste land wind up plainly like a garden. Isaiah 35:1b - "...The betray will be loaded with satisfaction and end up plainly like a rose." The place that is known for Israel resembles this now, so not quite the same as it was even a few years back.

17. Individuals will go places they have never gone and will know more than they have ever known some time recently. Daniel 12:4b: ".... Many will go all over and information will be to an ever increasing extent."

CHAPTER
FIFTEEN

The Anti-christ
(False-christ)

Just before Christ comes back to the earth with His Church, the Anti-christ (false christ) or the individual known as the antichrist, or the rebellious one will be offered energy to lead over all the earth. This time will be known as "the season of much inconvenience" or "the considerable tribulation," and will keep going for a long time.

There will be much awful and wrong done on the planet. This will be brought on by some false-christs. I John 2:18 let us know, "My youngsters, we are close to the apocalypse. You have heard that the false-christ is coming. Some false-christs have as of now come. This is the manner by which we know the apocalypse is close." Things will deteriorate in view of the genuine false-christ (The Anti-Christ) assuming control everything.

1. The Anti-Christ willl be the leader over all religions, governments, and cash of the world.

   Disclosure 13:7 - "It was permitted to battle

against the general population who have a place with God, and it had energy to disarm them. It had control over each family and each gathering of individuals and over individuals of each dialect and each country."

"The second wild creature was offered energy to offer life to the false god. This false god was the one that was made to resemble the primary wild creature. It was offered energy to talk. Each one of the individuals who did not love it would bite the dust."

Satan will be his manager, and he is likewise called the "wild creature." Revelation 13:2 - "The wild creature I saw was secured with spots. It had feet like those of a bear. It had a mouth like that of a lion. The snake-like creature gave this wild creature his own particular power and his own position of authority as lord.

The wild creature was given much power." In II Thessalonians 2:3 he is called "THE MAN OF SIN."

2. The false-christs employment will be to conflict with God, and all that is correct and great.

He will put himself up as though he is God.

He will have control over every one of the countries of the earth.

3. Nobody KNOWS WHEN THE FALSE-CHRIST WILL FIRST BE SEEN........

After the congregation is taken up to paradise and the Holy Spirit will at no time in the future be working with individuals on earth, the false-christ will begin his work immediately (II Thessalonians 2:6-8). Be that as it may, all Christians arre offered want to look to Christ, not the false-christ (Luke 21:28, 36).

4. The Anti-Christ (false-christ) will be permitted to come to rebuff the individuals who moved in the opposite direction of Christ and moved in the opposite direction of God's Word.

In II Thessalonians 2:11-12 - "Thus God will enable them to take after false lessons so they will trust a lie." "They will all be blameworthy as they remain before God since they needed to do what wasn't right."

CHAPTER
SIXTEEN

The Millennium Period
or
(The 1000 Years)

The 1,000 Year Period, 1,000 Time, or "The Millennium." In the initial seven verses of Revelation 20, 1,000 years is utilized six times.

1. PRE-MILLENNIUM

Premillennium implies that Christ will return before the 1,000 years. It shows that there is a 1,000 year time (or period) to come and that Christ will come back to earth before the 1,000 years. When He comes He and the Christians will manage the world. For the initial 300 years the early church instructed this.

2. AMILLENNIUM

Amillennium implies that the thousand years begun with the happening to Christ and experiences the entire New Testament time until the finish of this age. It implies that the Christians are presently administering with Christ and the individuals who have passed on are administering with Him up in paradise.

3. POSTMILLENNIUM

Postmillennium implies that Christ will come back to earth after the 1,000 year time is over.

Two imperative things will happen before the 1,000 year time.

1. The Battle Of Armageddon

This will be "A World War" against God and the Jews (Revelation 16:12-16). Christ will have control over the individuals who make war against God since He will descend from the sky and decimate the evil armed forces (Psalm 2; Isaiah 29:1-8; Joel 3:9; Zechariah 14:1-5; 14:12-15; Revelation 19:17-21).

2. The Nations Are Told If They Are Guilty.

After Christ wins the war of Armageddon, He will set up His Holy country on earth and assemble the countries before Him to state in the event that they are blameworthy (Matthew 25:31-46).

Some Other Things Will Happen

1. Satan will be tied and tossed into the gap without a base amid this 1,000 year time (Revelation 20:1-3).

2. The Christians who have been discharged from the graves will have their new pure bodies and will run with Christ on earth (Revelation 20:4).

3. The Sinful dead individuals won't be raised from the dead until the 1,000 year time is done (Revelation 20:5, 12).

4. The Jewish country will turn into a main force to be reckoned with amid this 1,000 year time (Zechariah 8:23).

The 1,000 year time and what will happen to the congregation, The Jews, and the countries:

1. The Christians will administer with Christ.

This would likewise imply that the individuals who languished over Christ amid the season of much inconvenience will administer with Christ. Disclosure 20:4 - "Then I saw honored positions. The individuals who were staying there were given the ability to state who is blameworthy. I saw the souls of the individuals who had been executed in light of the fact that they told about Jesus and lectured the Word of God.

They had not worshiped the wild creature or

his false god. They had not gotten the blemish on their temples or hands. They lived again and were pioneers alongside Christ for a long time."

2. God made a guarantee to David which has never been broken.

God guaranteed that the position of royalty of David sat to administer his country would be kept perpetually, and that David could never need a man to sit on it (II Samuel 7:11-17; Jeremiah 33:17). At the point when Christ cam to earth as a child in the town of Bethlehem, He had the privilege to take that honored position (Luke 1:32).

At the point when Christ will profit and govern for earth, He will utilize that same position of authority (Isaiah 9:6-7). The place of God that David manufactured will be assembled once more (Acts 15:16). The Jews will be a regarded and respected individuals on the earth (Zechariah 8:13).

3. The Battle of Armageddon

This will occur before the 1,000 year time and won't kill every one of the general population of the earth, yet just those armed forces that are battling in that fight. There will be individuals living in different parts of the world who will state Who Christ is.

Romans 14:11 - "The Holy Writings say, "As I live, says the Lord, each knew will bow down before me. What's more, every tongue will state that I am God.: "If each knee bows down before Christ, it doesn't imply that every one of these countries will put their trust in Christ.

It is one thing to bow down before Him and another to put one's trust in Him. On the off chance that any country keeps on battling against God and won't comply, that country will be rebuffed immediately (Zechariah 14:20-21).

The Reason For The 1,000 year time:

1. The 1,000 year time will be when God will test man the last time.

The 1,000 year time is not what Christians are anticipating. They (we) are anticipating the Holy City, the new Jerusalem (Revelation 21:9-22). This 1,000 year time will be when God will test man the last time. Things will be better then since Satan will be tied and off the beaten path and Christ will run the show.

2. The 1,000 year time will be an incredible time for the Jews.

Micah 4:6-7 - "In that day, says the Lord, "I will assemble the individuals who can't walk and the individuals who have been headed out, even those whom I have made to endure. I will make a fresh start with the individuals who can't walk. I will make a solid country of the individuals who have been dismissed. Also, the Lord will control over them in Mount Zion from that day until the end of time."

There will be peace over the earth(Isaiah 2:2-4; Micah 4:3-4). "There will be loads of cash, nourishment, and things (Isaiah 35). All creatures will get along well together (Isaiah 11:6-9). Christ will govern all things well. What He says and wills be correct (Isaiah 11:1-4).

After the 1,000 years Satan will be let free for some time. He will circumvent misleading the countries. Many individuals will tail Him. Not long after he will be tossed into the pool of flame (Revelation 20:10).

The earth and paradise will take off. In Revelation 20:11 - "Then I saw an awesome white position of royalty. I saw One Who sat on it. The earth and the paradise left Him in a rush and they could be found no more." This is, undoubtedly, what Peter expounded on in II Peter 3:7-10. At that point the immense white position of royalty where God sits will be seen, and the individuals who have never put their trust in Christ will be told they are liable (Revelation 20:11-15). The One Who sit on the colossal white position of royalty is Christ Jesus (John 5:22; Acts 17:31).

CHAPTER

SEVENTEEN

People Will Be Raised From The Dead

1. The 1,000 year won't be the apocalypse. Prior to the apocalypse different things will happen:

   A. The Christian will be raised from their graves when Christ wants the individuals who have put their trust in Him. I Corinthains 15:22-23 says, "All men will kick the bucket as Adam passed on. Be that as it may, each one of the individuals who have a place with Christ will be raised to new life. This is how it is:

Christ was raised from the dead first. At that point each one of the individuals who have a place with Christ will be raised from the dead when He comes back once more." (I Thessalonians 4:14-17). This will be before the 1,000 year time frame. It is known as the "Main Resurrection."

Disclosure 20:6 - "The individuals who are raised from the dead amid the first run through are upbeat and heavenly. The second passing has no control over them. They will be religious pioneers of God and Christ. They will be pioneers with Him for a long time.

B. The individuals who did not put their trust in Christ will be raised from their graves after the 1,000 year time frame is done. In Revelation 20:12-13 it says, "I saw all the dead individuals remaining before God. There were awesome individuals and little individuals. The was the book of life.

The dead individuals were told they were liable by what they had done as it is composed in the books. The ocean surrendered the dead individuals who were in it. Passing and damnation surrendered the dead individuals who were in them. Every one was told he was liable by what he had done."

2. The Chrisstian will remain before God before the 1,000 year time (Period). This is known as "The Judgment Seat Of Christ."

The Christian is not told he is blameworthy in light of the fact that God has as of now put that blame on His Son, Jesus Christ, on the cross. John 5:24 says, "Without a doubt, I let you know, any individual who hears My Word and puts his trust in Him Who sent Me has life that keeps going forever.

He won't be liable. He has as of now gone from death into life." His transgressions were dealt with at the cross, and by confidence in that work, he is free from the discipline of wrongdoing. In any case, all Christians must remain before Christ.

In II Corinthians 5:10 it says, "For every one of us must remain before Christ when He says who is blameworthy or not liable. Each of us will get pay for what he has done.

He will be paid for the great or the awful done while he lived in the body." This will happen when the congregation is taken up to meet the Lord noticeable all around. The reason Christians must remain before Christ around then is to tell what they have done in their work for Christ (Matthew 25:14-30; Luke 19:11-27).

The work of each Christian will be tried by flame. Some will be scorched to slag since they are just wood, feed, and grass. Different works will stand the test, and turned out as gold, silver, and stones worth much cash. Those whose works are consumed will be spared as though they were experiencing a fire. I Corinthians 3:12-15 says, "Now if a man works with wood or grass or straw, each man's work will end up plainly known. There will be a day when it will be tried by flame.

The fire will indicate what sort of work it is. On the off chance that a man expands on works that keeps going, he will get his compensation. On the off chance that his work is consumed, he will lose it. However he himself will be spared as though he were experiencing a fire." This will be a period when the Christian gets the compensation that is coming to him for his work.

Revelation 11:18b says, "........It is the ideal opportunity for the hirelings You possess who are the early ministers and the individuals who have a place with You to get the compensation that is coming to them. It is the ideal opportunity for the essential individuals and those not critical who respect your name to get the compensation that is coming to them. The time has come to devastate the individuals who have raised each sort of hell on earth."

Revelation 20:8b-9 says, "He will assemble them all together for war. There will be the same number of as the sand along the seashore. They will spread out over the earth and all around where God's kin are and around the city that is cherished. Fire will descend from God out of paradise and wreck them."

3. The Sinner will remain before God after the 1,000 year time (period). This is known as the considerable white position of royalty judgment.

The individual who is not a Christian will be told he is blameworthy on the grounds that his name is not composed in "The Book Of Life." In John 14:6 Jesus stated, "I am the Way, and The Truth, and the Life." No one can get to the Father aside from by Me." (Acts 4:12; I John 5:12).

The individuals who are told they are blameworthy willl languish discipline over transgression for eternity. There will never be a conclusion to the agony (Matthew 25:46; check 9:43, 48; Revelation 14:9-11).

The Place of that misery is called "the pool of flame" (Revelation 19:20; 20:10, 15).

It ought to be recalled that the pool of flame was made prepared for the "fallen angel" and "his blessed messengers," not for man (Matthew 25:41). In any case, the individuals who continue in the method for transgression must endure an indistinguishable discipline from the fiend and his holy messengers.

!!! Vital Note !!!

God need all men to be spared from the discipline of transgression. He said in Revelation 22:17b, "Let the person who needs to drink of the water of life, drink it. It is an unconditional present." And in II Peter 3:9b He says, "... The Lord does not need any individual to be rebuffed until the end of time." II Corinthians 6:2b says, "Now is the ideal time! Presently is the day of Salvation! Presently is the day to be saved!"(Isaiah 49:8).

CHAPTER
EIGHTEEN

The New Heaven And The New Earth

After the heavens and earth are destroyed with fire (II Peter 3:10) there will be new heavens and a new earth. (II Peter 3:13) This will be called "The Holy City" or "The New Jerusalem."

It will be a far better place than man can think of. Only what is right and good will be there. There will be no more death, or sorrow, or crying, or pain. Everyone will be worshiping God. There will be no more night there. It will be a new home for all those who have put their trust in Christ and have been saved from the punishment of their sins (Revelation 21; 22:5).

He Who tells these things says, "Yes, I am coming soon! "Let it be so." Come, Lord Jesus." (Revelation 22:20)

BIBLIOGRAPHY

The Holy Bible (1901) The American Standard Version. Nashville, TN.: Thomas Nelson (used by permission)

The Holy Bible (1964) The Authorized King James Version. Chicago, Ill.: J.G. Ferguson Company

The Holy Bible (1969) The New Life Version. Canby, OH.: Christian Literature International (used by permission)

The New Life Study Testament (1986) New Life Version. Canby, OH.: Christian Literature International (used by permission)

The Wycliff Bible Commentary (1968) Chicago, Ill.: The Moody Bible Institute Of Chicago

ABOUT THE AUTHOR

The Reverend Dr. John Thomas Wylie is one who has dedicated his life to the work of God's Service, the service of others; and being a powerful witness for the Gospel of Our Lord and Savior Jesus Christ. Dr. Wylie was called into the Gospel Ministry June 1979, whereby in that same year he entered The American Baptist College of the American Baptist Theological Seminary, Nashville, Tennessee.

As a young Seminarian, he read every book available to him that would help him better his understanding of God as well as God's plan of Salvation and the Christian Faith. He made a commitment as a promising student that he would inspire others as God inspires him. He understood early in his ministry that we live in times where people question not only who God is; but whether miracles are real, whether or not man can make a change, and who the enemy is or if the enemy truly exists.

Dr. Wylie carried out his commitment to God, which has been one of excellence which led to his earning his Bachelors of Arts in Bible/ Theology/Pastoral Studies. Faithful and obedient to the call of God, he continued to matriculate in his studies earning his Masters of Ministry from Emmanuel Bible College, Nashville, Tennessee & Emmanuel Bible College, Rossville, Georgia. Still, inspired to please the Lord and do that which is well – pleasing in the Lord's sight, Dr. Wylie recently on March 2006, completed his Masters of Education degree with a concentration in Instructional Technology earned at The American Intercontinental University, Holloman Estates, Illinois. Dr. Wylie also previous to this, earned his Education Specialist Degree from Jones International University, Centennial, Colorado and his Doctorate of Theology from The Holy Trinity College and Seminary, St. Petersburg, Florida.

Dr. Wylie has served in the capacity of pastor at two congregations in Middle and Southern Tennessee, as well as served as an Evangelistic Preacher, Teacher, Chaplain, Christian Educator, and finally a published author, writer of many great inspirational Christian Publications such as his first publication: *"Only One God: Who*

Is He?" – published August 2002 via formally 1st books library (which is now AuthorHouse Book Publishers located in Bloomington, Indiana & Milton Keynes, United Kingdom) which caught the attention of **The Atlanta Journal Constitution Newspaper.**

ABOUT THE BOOK

It is the plan of this publication to: "Go ye into all the world and broadcast, report, teach and proclaim the Gospel." It is the obligation of each Christian. As Christians, we are called to speak to and display Christ. It is here that we concentrate on the Biblical record of what God's Word teaches about Christ.

Why the Bible? Since it is the Christian's Holy Book from God (Scriptures) in which we discover a record of what God has done and declared in history for his picked individuals and for all of humankind, and what God requires of men in light of what he has done that they might be saved.

It is the main answer for the wrongdoing (sin) and despondency of humanity and the main route for compromise with God for everlasting life (Romans 6:23; John 3:36; 3:16).

Majority of scriptures are taken from the King James Version, The New Life Version, American Standard Version, and "Paraphrased," unless otherwise indicated.

Reverend Dr. John Thomas Wylie

Printed in the United States
By Bookmasters